Original title:
Life: Where's the Instruction Booklet?

Author: Rafael Sterling
ISBN HARDBACK: 978-1-80566-231-0
ISBN PAPERBACK: 978-1-80566-526-7

The Mystique of the Unscripted

Woke up this morning all bright and spry,
Checked my manual, it says 'Oh my!'
No buttons to press, no instructions in sight,
Just a cup of coffee to fuel my flight.

I asked the wise owl for a piece of advice,
He hooted and laughed, said 'Just roll the dice!'
With every odd turn, chaos won't cease,
Welcome to the circus, enjoy the peace!

Finding Wisdom in the Mistakes

Tried to bake cookies, added salt like a pro,
Turns out it tasted more like a no-show.
My friends took one bite, then ran for the door,
'Next recipe, please!' they hollered, 'No more!'

Each blunder I make, I gather some gold,
From spilled milk to burnt toast, the stories unfold.
They say laugh it off, it's a part of the jest,
At least now I know, I'm a cooking unrest.

A Journey Through Unmarked Trails

With a map made of napkins, I set out to roam,
Lost in the wild, far away from home.
A squirrel stole my sandwich, oh what a thief,
I consulted a fern for some wise, green relief.

Up a tree, I climbed, to find a great view,
But tripped on my shoelace, and fell out of the blue.
Found wisdom in bruises and laughter in tears,
Here's to the journey, despite all my fears!

Stumbling Towards Enlightenment

They said 'Walk with purpose!' I took that to heart,
But then tripped on my shoelace, an awkward start.
I laughed with a pigeon, who found it quite cute,
As I dusted myself off in my dorky suit.

Each misstep a lesson, like a comedic play,
Falling forward is just my own quirky way.
So here's to the stumbles, the laughs in the mess,
Who needs a handbook when chaos's the best?

The Shadows of What We Didn't Learn

We stumble through this quirky maze,
Searching for the reasoned ways.
A manual lost, a charter gone,
We laugh and learn to carry on.

The wise may chuckle at our plight,
In jumbled lines we find our might.
With every misstep, we embrace the fun,
Collecting stories, one by one.

Tales from the Unwritten Chapters.

There's wisdom lingering in the air,
Invisible guides that never care.
They tease us with their cryptic jokes,
As we slip and slide like clumsy folks.

Each chapter adds a twist or turn,
Yet still, there's so much left to learn.
With laughter echoing through each page,
We dance along, but feel no age.

Navigating the Uncharted Pages

Maps are scribbled on the back of dreams,
Unfolding stories in quirky themes.
We plot our course with every blunder,
Finding joy through the chaos we wander.

In guides unwritten, we explore with glee,
Each misadventure makes us free.
With humor brightening every dip,
We sail through life on a joyful trip.

The Manual of Unspoken Wisdom

A crumpled note, no answers found,
Yet laughs explode in merry sound.
We grasp the lessons, oh so sly,
In the silence of the questioning why.

Each unwritten law, a playful jest,
In searching deep, we find the best.
So giggle softly, take a chance,
The manual mocks us with its dance.

Whispers of an Unexplained Journey

In a world of maps with no directions,
We stumble on paths of odd connections.
My GPS says, 'recalculating now,'
As I wander confused, questioning how.

Cats avoid puddles, dogs chase their tails,
While fish dream of flying, exploring the trails.
Instructions are hidden in giggles and sighs,
As monkeys throw bananas, raising our cries.

Crafting Meaning from Chaos

Once I sought wisdom from a magic eight ball,
But it only replied, 'Ask again, call!'
With crayons and scribbles, I sketch my own fate,
In a circus of thoughts, I open the gate.

On Tuesday, I'm serious, Thursday quite wacky,
Each moment's a riddle that feels so tacky.
I laugh with the flowers, I dance with the breeze,
While ants hold a meeting, discussing their cheese.

The Language of Uncertainty

If socks have a voice, they'd say I'm alone,
While keys roam the house, claiming it's their throne.
I tried to decode a cat's puzzled stare,
But I was met with a yawn and some hair.

Pancakes are round, but life's edges are square,
Tangled in thoughts, I twirl through the air.
Each day is a puzzle, each laugh a new piece,
As I chase after moments, hoping for peace.

On the Boundaries of Understanding

With fruit loops in hand, I ponder the stars,
Why do zebras wear stripes and not fancy cars?
The answers are tangled in laughter and glee,
As I play hide and seek with my thoughts, set them free.

Cherry trees giggle as breeze sings a tune,
While squirrels hold conferences by light of the moon.
I guess I'll just wander with joy on my face,
For the journey's the treasure, not just the place.

The Dance of Serendipitous Moments

Twists and turns, oh what a show,
Stumbling here, just go with the flow.
Laughing at plans that all went wrong,
Find the beat, we'll dance along.

Like a jester wearing mismatched shoes,
We trip and tumble, it's hard to lose.
Each slip a chance to spin and glide,
In this chaotic, joyous ride.

So let's twirl through the absurd and wild,
Embrace the dance, we're all just children.
A misstep here, a little fall,
In this funny tango, we have it all.

The Hidden Treasures of Failure

Failed attempts, like buried gold,
Gems disguised, their stories untold.
Falling flat, a hearty laugh,
Who knew mistakes could embody craft?

Like pancakes that refuse to flip right,
Stuck to the pan, oh what a sight!
Yet syrup flows, sweet on the plate,
Turns out failures can also be great.

So here's to the stumbles we make,
Each misadventure, a chance to awake.
With humor we gather, treasure in hand,
Embrace the blunders, together we stand.

A Poetry of Unfolding Journeys

Maps all crumpled, where's the road?
With every wrong turn, new stories flowed.
Like a pot of soup, a hodgepodge of spice,
Every detour adds a little more nice.

Oh, the strangers we meet on the way,
With quirks and tales that make us sway.
A merry band of lost souls seeking,
Finding joy in the funny and the leaking.

So we trek on, with chuckles in tow,
Not knowing just where we will go.
With every miscalculation we embrace,
In this poem of twists, it's a happy race.

Where Roads Converge and Diverge

Fork in the road, which way to go?
Toss a coin, or just steal the show.
One path leads to mundane and plain,
The other to sunshine mixed with rain.

We wave to the left, then swerve to the right,
In this comic adventure, we take flight.
With giggles and grumbles, we dance and spin,
Wherever we end, let the fun begin!

It's here that we gather our fumbles and laughs,
Navigating chaos like quirk-filled staffs.
At the junction of roads, come join the circus,
With each silly turn, it's all worth it, circus!

The Pattern of Windblown Leaves

In autumn's dance, leaves whirl and twirl,
Like socks in a dryer, they give a twirl.
Instructions unread, they float to the ground,
Wondering aloud, 'Did we make a sound?'

Branches reach out, with a 'what's the deal?'
Whispering secrets, none of us feel.
A squirrel holds court, with acorns so bright,
Confidently claiming his spot for the night.

Sometimes they assemble, a jumbled confetti,
While gusts of wind think they're far more petty.
Spinning and swirling, a chaotic affair,
One leaf shouts, "Hey, I never signed up for this air!"

But soon the chill comes, and they give a sigh,
No rules to abide, just letting them fly.
As they blanket the ground, a warm, crunchy quilt,
They chuckle, "We're free! No need to feel guilt!"

The Lost Art of Listening to Silence

In a world filled with buzz and endless noise,
Where chatty machines drown out all the joys.
We search for the calm beneath all the chatter,
While a wise old frog croaks, 'Does it really matter?'

A bear in the woods naps, dreaming of fish,
While nearby a bee forgets what to wish.
'Excuse me,' it buzzes, 'What are you selling?'
The bear snorts, 'Just quiet—got time for a yelling?'

The clock ticks away, pets snooze in repose,
While Wi-Fi alerts us—the signal that glows.
"Let's silence our phones," we hopeful declare,
And hear 'neath our breath, the soft sigh of air.

But silence is tricky, like socks in a wash,
It vanishes quickly, like a breath with a posh.
Yet here in this stillness, a funny thought lingers:
Sometimes you find peace, just removing the fingers!

A Traveler's Diary of Discoveries

I packed my bags, left home for gold,
Found a map that's tattered, and stories told.
Got lost in circles, what a silly chase,
A signpost points, yet I'm in the wrong place.

Chased after treasures, but they all were fake,
Ordered the soup, it turned out to be cake.
Every step forward, I stumbled and tripped,
But every wrong turn, my spirit just skipped.

The locals laughed, said I looked confused,
I bought a guidebook and misused the clues.
With a smile, I wandered, forgetting the fuss,
As GPS said, "You've arrived! Just not with us!"

In the end, I learned what no words could teach,
That adventures abound beyond the right reach.
So pack the laughter, forget the stress,
In this open world, who needs to impress?

The Poetry of Trial and Error

I rolled out of bed with dreams in my head,
Thought I'd make breakfast and end up well-fed.
Burnt the toast, set off a smoke alarm,
Turns out I can't cook – who knew it was harm?

Tried to plant flowers, thought I'd be a pro,
Watered them daily, they decided to grow.
But instead of blossoms, I got weeds galore,
Not quite what I wanted, but what's life for?

I signed up for classes, thought I'd learn art,
With paint on my fingers, I thought I was smart.
The canvas yelled back, "What's that supposed to be?"
I laughed at my masterpiece, a sight to see.

Every mishap a lesson, wrapped in a joke,
Mistakes are the punchlines when life starts to poke.
So I pencil in laughter, erase all the fear,
In this grand comedy, I'll shout, "Encore, dear!"

Footprints on Untrodden Soil

Stomped through the mud, left prints like a clown,
In a field of confusion, I tumbled right down.
Every path I chose was a riddle, not clear,
Yet I pranced around, filled with cheeky cheer.

Wore mismatched shoes, oh what a delight,
Fell off my bike, claimed I'd flown for a flight.
With laughter in the air and dirt on my face,
These goofs are the stories that time can't erase.

Danced with my shadow in the glow of the moon,
Stepped on my own foot and then sang a tune.
Every misstep a rhythm, every fall worth a cheer,
In this crazy adventure, I've nothing to fear.

So I'll mark these moments, with giggles and glee,
In the soil of wonder, my heart's running free.
Embrace all the blunders, let laughter unfold,
For each step I take is a story retold.

Navigating from the Heart

My compass was broken, just spinning around,
Set sail to discover what's lost, what's profound.
A map made of scribbles, directions from glee,
Followed my heart, it led me to tea.

Thought I could dance on a road made of dreams,
Twisted my ankle, fell into streams.
With a grin on my face, I splashed in the muck,
Found joy in the stumble, who knew I could luck?

Hearts don't need GPS or fairytale guides,
Just a dash of madness, where laughter abides.
So I'll sail through the nonsense, with joy as my chart,
For the best of adventures are navigated by heart.

In the end, it's the moments that make spirits rise,
A journey of chuckles under bright-painted skies.
Let's toast to the wobbles, to laughter and fun,
For the map of our heart is where journeys are won.

The Odyssey of Imperfection

In the quest for a perfect day,
I tripped on my own shoelace play.
Should've read the manual, it seems,
But instead, I'm lost in daydreams.

I asked the stars for some advice,
They blinked at me, not once, but twice.
With every step, I dance and swerve,
It's clear the rules I do not observe.

Adventures hide in silly holes,
When cookies crumble, laughter rolls.
My map's a doodle, my compass spins,
Who knew life's chaos would wear such grins?

So here's to blunders, slaps, and cheer,
For every fail brings a new frontier.
With snacks in hand and smiles so wide,
I'm navigating with humor as my guide.

The Unscripted Symphony

Tuning forks lay scattered around,
In this orchestra, chaos is sound.
No sheet music, just whims and giggles,
Playing tunes with our little wiggles.

The conductor's absent, lost in thought,
We make music from mishaps we've caught.
A trumpet with a croak, a violin squeaks,
Yet somehow it's magic that speaks.

Dancing to rhythms that wobble and dart,
Each solo a mash-up of heart and art.
When notes clash, we chuckle and sway,
For in this racket, we find our way.

So grab a friend, let the notes collide,
In this grand mess, let our joy reside.
The symphony's ours, whirling and bright,
Unscripted and wild, oh what a sight!

Whims of Wandering Souls

Off we go, with maps upside down,
Our compass points to the nearest town.
With snacks packed high and hats askew,
Who needs directions? We've got a view!

Chasing sunsets with giggling glee,
We'll take the path that's less, not free.
Each wrong turn sparks a tale to trade,
Finding happiness in missteps made.

Dear wanderers, lost but so alive,
With every hiccup, we learn to thrive.
We're digital nomads without a plan,
Just free spirits and a sandwich can.

So raise a toast to the paths unknown,
In this grand adventure, we've fully grown.
With laughter as our guiding star,
We'll wander together, near and far.

Chronicles of the Unseen Guide

A book of rules, what a bore,
I'd rather dance on the grocery floor.
With a flick of the wrist, I try to steer,
But somehow I ended up with a deer!

Lost in a world of quirky signs,
I bump into fate like it's all just fine.
Who needs a guide when you've got your wit,
And a funny friend to share a bit?

Each twist and turn's a comedy show,
With pratfalls that steal the whole tableau.
Forget the manual, let's live it up,
With soda spills from our overflowing cup.

So here's to the wisdom that's often not seen,
In this chaotic tale, we're free and keen.
With laughter lighting up the dimmed sky,
We write our own chapters, you and I.

Wandering with No Destination

I wake each day, a map unwritten,
My shoes are tied, but thoughts are smitten.
Coffee spills, my compass gone,
Yet forward I dance, with a half-baked song.

What's left or right? Who even knows?
I laugh with trees that sprout like prose.
The sun goes down, while my snacks run dry,
A squirrel waves as it passes by.

My GPS thinks I'm a rolling joke,
Yet here I am, just a wandering bloke.
Stumbling onward, humor intact,
With no real answers, just whimsical acts.

The Forgotten Guidelines

Yesterday I found a guidebook worn,
But the pages were dusty, the cover all torn.
It called for pragmatism, but I just yawned,
I'd rather a dance with the hippopotamond.

Rules like 'don't run' made me want to race,
Why march in queues when there's a wild place?
I tiptoe through puddles and jump just for fun,
Forgotten guidelines, oh well, who needs one?

Instructions for coffee? More like a mystery,
Not brew it strong, but let it flow free.
So cheers to the chaos, the joy and the jest,
For finding my chaos is better than rest.

Straying from the Beaten Path

I took a left when the sign said right,
Now I'm lost beneath the starlit night.
Embracing detours like a surface-level thrill,
Spider webs gloss my chocolate spill.

A hot air balloon? Why not give chase!
With laughter and snacks, I'm a lost little ace.
Navigating puddles and friendly cat calls,
I'm straying from paths, oh the glory befalls!

Who needs a trail, when I have my tunes?
With moonlight guiding, all secrets are runes.
So let's revel in paths not drawn on a sheet,
I seek the odd joys, as my soles take a beat.

Finding Clarity in Confusion

In a world of chaos, I trip and I slide,
Yet giggles arise, like confetti, my guide.
With socks mismatched and my hair a great mess,
I wade through my thoughts, but I've got finesse.

Though clouds seem dark, I wear shades of cheer,
What's wrong with mishaps, if laughter's near?
A puzzle unsolved, with pieces that flee,
Yet clarity whispers, "Just let it be me."

We fumble and tumble, oh what a sight!
Confusion's a friend, so let's hold it tight.
I'll embrace every quirk, each little flaw,
And find wisdom wrapped in a humorous awe.

The Calligraphy of Experience

I scribble notes on napkins,
With thoughts of where to go.
The ink smudges laugh at me,
Yet wisdom starts to grow.

The margins hold my secrets,
And doodles fill the page.
Each error tells a story,
In this spontaneous stage.

Coffee spills, a text surprise,
While I'm searching for the way.
I find the best directions,
Are the ones that lead astray.

So here's to bad handwriting,
And moments full of fun.
For every misadventure,
Is a lesson just begun.

The Art of Broken Roads

I took a trip to nowhere,
The GPS went blind.
With every turn I'm bouncing,
Uncertainty aligned.

Potholes act as surprises,
And speed bumps make me dance.
Each wrong turn I encounter,
Is a chance for new romance.

No map leads to perfection,
Just laughter in the breeze.
I'll paint my path in colors,
No one knows, but me with ease.

As asphalt turns to gravel,
And tires start to squeak,
I'll cherish each misstep,
For they're all part of the peak.

Embracing Uncertainty's Embrace

In a world full of maybe,
I've learned to say, 'Why not?'
The answers hide in shadows,
Or just around the plot.

Mistakes become my buddies,
With laughter as a tune.
So let's dance with the unknown,
Underneath the moon.

I open doors to nowhere,
And walk on paths of chance.
Each stumble has its glory,
And gives the heart a bounce.

So here's to all the 'what ifs,'
And 'oops' that come my way.
For in this silly tango,
I find the joys of play.

A Blueprint Written in Sand

I sketched my dreams on seashore,
With waves that washed it clean.
Each outline held a promise,
Of what could have been seen.

As castles made of sponges,
Are destined to erode,
I learn to trust the moments,
That shift along the road.

With every drifting grain,
A lesson in disguise.
I laugh when plans are wiped out,
While searching for the wise.

So let the tide come rolling,
While I dance on shifting sands.
For in this fleeting blueprint,
I create with clumsy hands.

Unfolding Without a Blueprint

We wake up each day in a whirl,
With socks that clash and hair in a twirl.
No manual for breakfast, just guess and pour,
And wonder if coffee's love's greatest lore.

We bumble through plans like a cat in a hat,
Inventing our rules, with a whimsy spat.
Instructions get lost in giggles and sighs,
As we scribble our dreams in the clouded skies.

Echoes of Untold Stories

In the park, we stumble over our shoes,
Chasing the echoes of what to choose.
The bench is our throne, we regale with art,
On how to not trip and still win at heart.

With laughter as glue for our patched-up tales,
We navigate life like it's full of scales.
Every hiccup's a chapter that's worthy of cheer,
For what's better than laughing when the path's unclear?

The Puzzle Without a Picture

A thousand pieces scattered about,
No corner in sight, filled with doubt.
Colors all jumbled, where does this piece go?
Yet the fun's in the challenge, don't you know?

With each wacky twist, we find our own way,
Pretending to know what we're meant to say.
So we fit the odd shapes with a chuckle or two,
Adventurers laughing, what else can we do?

Embracing the Uncharted Path

Maps are boring, so let's take a jump,
Off the beaten trail, into a bump!
With snacks as our guide and friends by our side,
We'll navigate chaos with reckless pride.

Step by step, we dance through the mess,
Wearing mismatched shoes, we still feel blessed.
Each twist and each turn comes wrapped in a grin,
For the joy's in the journey, let the fun begin!

Stories Beneath the Surface

In the depths, a fish wears specs,
It reads the tales on sunken decks.
The mermaids giggle, flip their hair,
While turtles ponder—do they care?

A clam once wrote a guide, you see,
On how to sip your morning tea.
But pearls are shy, they hide too well,
Their wisdom lost in ocean swell.

Crabs clutch secrets with their claws,
While octopuses applaud with pause.
Yet in the tides, we dance in glee,
Like jellyfish at a jamboree.

So here's the scoop from deep and wide,
In each crevice, laughter hides.
With every splash, a tale is spun,
Underwater antics, oh what fun!

The Craft of Embracing Chaos

With socks on hands and socks on feet,
I juggle fruit while I take a seat.
The cat is plotting, eyeing my toast,
While my coffee sings—what a lively boast!

A recipe calls for sugar and spice,
But I toss in pickles—oh, isn't that nice?
The blender's whirling, I dance in place,
As the neighbors all stare—what a kooky face!

My calendar's filled with mystery dates,
I gear up for lunch, but it's time for crates.
With every mistake, I learn to sway,
And tiptoe through mayhem, come what may.

So grab your chaos, embrace the noise,
Create a ruckus, oh what joys!
For in the zany, we find our way,
To laugh and giggle through the fray!

The Compass of Intuition

A squirrel debates which path to roam,
While I consult my fridge for home.
The toast says 'yes', the pickle says 'no',
In this culinary circus, who's the star of the show?

The map is upside down, I'm still quite lost,
My compass broke, and what a cost!
Each step I take, I trip and fall,
But I swear I heard a muffin call!

Feet in the puddles, I do the twist,
Dodging the raindrops, oh, what bliss!
Trust in the gut, my tummy knows best,
Adventure is calling; I'll take a wild guess.

So if you find yourself astray,
Just follow the whimsy of your day.
For every detour hides a delight,
Just wander on, from morning to night!

Exploring the Abyss of the Unknown

A shadow whispers, 'What's down there?'
I peer into voids without a care.
A sock monster laughs, 'Looking for me?'
With every corner turned, it's a wacky spree!

With a rubber chicken and a map of cheese,
I wade through mysteries with utmost ease.
The night hums tunes, so eerie yet bright,
Each step reveals absurdity in sight.

The abyss is friendly, it winks and grins,
While the echoes tease, and the fun begins.
So hold on tight, it's a hilarity ride,
Through giggles and jumbles, let heartbeams guide.

In the depths of unknown, we find a cheer,
With laughter and joy, we'll persevere.
So gather your courage, step into the play,
In the absurd abyss, let's frolic away!

The Map of Heartfelt Wanderings

We roam with maps that make no sense,
Direction's lost in sheer pretense.
With a compass that points to spaghetti,
And a GPS that acts all petty.

We follow paths where squirrels laugh,
Playing tic-tac-toe on a whacky graph.
Each turn we take feels like a jest,
Should have packed a guide for this wild quest.

But every stumble brings a grin,
Like tripping over thoughts within.
We'll dance through mischief, come what may,
In this mapless journey, we'll find our way!

So here's to the routes that aren't defined,
To find our treasures, sweetly aligned.
For laughter's the key, our greatest friend,
As we wander, oh, let the fun not end!

Unsung Melodies of Existence

We hum a tune no one can hear,
In silent notes, we persevere.
With harmonies of quirks amassed,
We compose a song for the outcast.

Oh, the choir of confused bees,
Buzzing around with utmost glee.
Each misstep's a rhythmic clap,
Who needs sheet music for this scrapbook app?

As octopuses play the violin,
We wonder where this laugh begins.
Each note strikes loud like thunder's call,
In jest we flourish, in joy, we fall.

Here's to the symphony of our mess,
In every discord, we find success.
So let's dance to verses we create,
In this wacky world, we celebrate!

The Wisdom of Uncharted Waters

We sail the seas with leaky boats,
Where wisdom floats like dingy coats.
With maps that show "X marks the fun,"
And gulls that drop advice—it's all a pun!

The waves will tease, the winds will sigh,
As dolphins giggle and fish comply.
Each wave's a riddle, each splash a cheer,
Navigating chaos is why we're here!

With treasure chests of silly dreams,
And beaches glistening with ice cream streams.
We'll dive for pearls but swim through jest,
In the ocean's womb, we're truly blessed.

So raise the sails and let's embark,
On this voyage bright, let's leave our mark.
For wisdom's in the jest we glide,
In uncharted waters, we'll take the ride!

Discoveries Within the Labyrinth

In a maze where socks disappear,
We hunt for shoes and pizza, dear.
Each corner turns a wild surprise,
Like trying on new, ridiculous ties.

The walls speak riddles; the floor's a game,
Lost in thoughts that don't feel the same.
A snack break here could save the day,
But will the cheese run away? Hooray!

With mirrors that giggle and doors that squeak,
We meander through the quirky peak.
Oh, the fun is in finding our way,
In this make-believe, we dance and play.

So grab a friend and take a leap,
In this labyrinth, secrets we keep.
For even when lost, we laugh and find,
The joy in wonders, joyfully entwined!

Chaos and Clarity

In a world where plans go astray,
We dance like squirrels in disarray.
Maps are useless, they twist and bend,
Just laugh it off, and call it a trend.

Expectations pile, like laundry high,
We question the stars, and wonder why.
Yet amidst the mess, we grin and play,
For chaos can bring a bright new day.

In Search of Missing Pages

I flipped through the chapters, what's wrong with this
tome?
It skips over wisdom and leaves me alone.
Each party I throw, feels more like a quiz,
Who knew adulting was such a busy whizz?

I reached for the fine print, but all I found,
Were doodles of cats and a joke that's quite sound.
So I laugh at the mishaps, take life in streaks,
And savor the fun in the scattered weeks.

The Unwritten Manual

They say there's a manual, hidden away,
But it's lost in the couch, under crumbs of play.
I'm winging it daily, with dog-eared dreams,
Finding joy in the journey, it's never as it seems.

Instructions are boring, I'll tell you right now,
Embrace every hiccup, that's my solemn vow.
With every wrong turn, a new lesson blooms,
Who needs a guidebook? Just grab the brooms!

Navigating the Unknown

I set my course by the stars up above,
But they wink and they giggle, it's not what they love.
Google can guide me, but who needs the app?
I'll take a wrong turn, and there's still a clap.

Every route I choose feels whimsically mad,
But trust in the journey makes my heart glad.
So here's to the fumbles, let the fun roll,
For in every misstep, there's joy for the soul.

The Archive of Missteps

In every stumble, there's a laugh,
A manual lost, in the wrong half.
I've navigated messes, no map in hand,
Each blunder a treasure in this strange land.

With socks unmatched, I strut and preen,
I trip on flat ground, it's quite the scene.
The GPS whispers, 'Just recalculate,'
But all I can do is scoff and wait.

Recipes call for zest, I bring on the zest,
Burnt offerings serve, at my uninvited fest.
Turn left at chaos, then right at the wrong,
Singin' a ditty to my own silly song.

Yet laughter grows stronger in each misfire,
Each detour I take builds my comedy choir.
Who needs a guide when the journey's a jest?
With every odd twist, I am truly blessed.

The Beautiful Mistake

A dish served cold, my meal à la doom,
An artful creation of chaos in bloom.
I painted my walls with hues of delight,
Turns out it was ketchup—I lost that fight.

In fashion mismatched, I swagger with pride,
My shirt's on the outside, my pants want to hide.
Who's to declare what's a snazzy mistake?
Even a bore might just jump in the lake!

Directions all wrong, but the views are so fine,
The wrong turn led me to the bright sunshine.
With every mishap, there's beauty to find,
Each oops in the plot leaves a mark in my mind.

So let's toast to the errors that color our days,
The blunders that dance in so many ways.
May the beautiful mess be cherished, not grim,
For each tiny slip, let the laughter begin.

Riddles Beneath the Surface

Oh, the riddles we weave in our scrabble for sense,
Questions that tickle, yet leave us on suspense.
A sock in the fridge, and a cat in my hat,
What's wrong with my picture? Perhaps I'm just fat.

Puzzles unsolved float in the air,
I ponder their meaning almost everywhere.
Why do we stumble on things that were clear?
Is the answer elusive or just full of cheer?

With giggles and snorts, I untangle the twist,
Every awkward dilemma is impossible to miss.
In laughter we seek the sense out of plight,
Navigating the day, even wrong turns feel right.

So let's play with the questions, sip tea with our doubts,
Finding joy in the chaos is what this is about.
For every riddle wrapped snug in absurd,
There's laughter among us, unspoken yet heard.

Parables of the Unsung

Gather 'round, friends, for a tale intertwined,
Of wisdom in blunders, so profound yet blind.
A hero dismissed in his mismatched attire,
Chasing the sunset, ignited by fire.

With forks in the road and spaghetti on feet,
Our merry misfortune becomes our treat.
In lessons misunderstood, we argue, we jest,
The greatest wisdom's hidden in laughter's quest.

Let's gather the stories of moments we fray,
The hat's on the dog, it's a glorious play.
With each funny moment, though tough it may seem,
The parables dance like a wild, silly dream.

So raise up your glass to the blunders we keep,
To the unsung parables —the memories steep.
In a world full of chaos, we find our true song,
Embrace every misstep—let's all sing along!

Harmonies of the Unpredictable

In the morning, socks don't match,
Coffee spills, oh what a catch!
A fish jumps, and I just stare,
Wait, was that supposed to scare?

Pants are tight; today's a breeze,
Is it summer? Or just tease?
The cat thinks it runs the show,
While I'm here just figuring flow.

Maps get lost; directions flee,
Turns out, I'm on a shopping spree.
Dinner burns to crispy ash,
Who knew cooking could be such a crash?

Judging by the mismatched scenes,
Every day, a balance beams.
With clumsy kicks and laughter loud,
This wild dance, I'm still so proud.

The Journal of Incomplete Stories

I started a tale with great flair,
But alas, I just lost my hair!
A hero's quest to find a sock,
Turns into a pet rock mock.

Oh, the plots I've left behind,
A book of blanks, a thoughtful find.
Once wrote about a charming frog,
He turned into a lazy dog.

Epic battles, cardboard swords,
But which is which? I lost my cords.
In every chapter, just a pause,
Who needs a reason, or a cause?

Ending here, it feels as right,
I laugh at stories that take flight.
Each line a puzzle, messy bliss,
In my clumsy tales, I find my kiss.

Embracing Life's Mosaic of Moments

A puzzle piece without a plan,
But hey, I'm still a quirky fan.
Sunshine dips, and rainbows come,
Mix it all, beat like a drum.

I wore my shoes on the wrong feet,
But whistled tunes, oh, what a treat!
In splashes bright and colors bold,
Every day's a story told.

Ice cream drips, runs down my hand,
A sticky mess, just like I planned.
And laughter bubbles everywhere,
Moments captured in the air.

So let them dance, so let them play,
These patchwork scenes, a grand ballet.
In every tick, a giggle sings,
A crazy quilt of joyous things.

The Art of Unsynchronized Steps

In the dance, I missed the cue,
Two left feet, who needs just two?
The rhythm skips, like a slinky fall,
But in my heart, I hear the call.

Watch me waltz, or trip, or slide,
A circus act without a guide.
The beat goes on, I jump and twirl,
Flailing limbs, a whirling swirl.

Oh wait, was that your toe I crushed?
With all my grace, my feet are flushed.
A pirouette turned to a stumble,
And now my ego starts to crumble.

Yet here I laugh, and give a spin,
In every fumble lies the win.
One unplanned step leads to delight,
Embrace this dance, embrace the night.

Lessons in the Everyday

I tripped over my own two feet,
A lesson learned, quite discreet.
Like socks that always mismatch,
Is this a style, or just a catch?

I poured juice into the wrong glass,
Was it a moment or a class?
The toast jumped, oh what a flight!
Breakfast chaos, what a sight!

The cat scratched at my brand new chair,
"Is this a pet, or a teddy bear?"
I chuckled as it stole my seat,
Oh, this school of fun is sweet.

So here's to errors, big and small,
With each misstep, I stand tall.
The rules we bend, the paths we weave,
In every blunder, there's joy to leave.

When the Guide is Absent

With no directions, I hit a wall,
A treasure map? Just a shopping mall!
I asked a goose for some advice,
It quacked, "Oh dear, it's not so nice!"

The manual's lost, I can't locate,
Did I drop it, or is it fate?
Who knew plants could make me sneeze?
A guide could help, just, please!

Turning left instead of right,
I ended up in a dance-off fight.
"Just follow the rules!" someone yelled,
But in my world, chaos is upheld!

So I'll wander, laugh and grin,
Without a guide, I still will win.
Each twist and turn is quite a spree,
In freedom lies the best of me.

Scribbles in the Margins

In my notebook, doodles bloom,
Of clouds and cats and endless zoom.
A recipe for gumbo galore,
Made soup instead, oh what a score!

Notes from class that lost their way,
"Don't mix colors," said a wise gray.
Yet here I am, in colors bright,
Splattered splashes, pure delight!

A shopping list turned into art,
To buy some eggs, but where to start?
Instead, I grabbed some candy bars,
Who knew food goals had such stars?

So let the scribbles guide my days,
In chaotic, comical, funny ways.
Amid the mess, I find my spark,
In every blunder, I leave my mark.

The Mapless Journey

With no map in hand, I set to roam,
Each step, a chance to build a home.
I took a right at the barking dog,
Found a shortcut through thick fog.

Wandered into a strange café,
Where the coffee served had much to say.
It spilled on me, a warm surprise,
Just like the laughter in my eyes!

In gardens wild, I lost my shoe,
Dancing barefoot with morning dew.
"Oh, don't you fret," said a bumblebee,
"Just enjoy the buzz, come dance with me!"

So off I wander, brave and spry,
With no directions, I will fly.
The journey's fun, let's make it bright,
In the mapless dance, we'll find our light.

Whispers of the Unfamiliar

In the morning, I lost my shoe,
Forgot the milk, the cat just flew.
Coffee spills, my toast's on fire,
Instructions, please! My skills retire.

I tripped on socks, my pants did fall,
A juggling act, I fear no brawl.
The dog just laughed, he found it fun,
Where's the manual? I've just begun!

Dinner is served, but what's that smell?
Is it the fish or just a shell?
Family meeting, the question's clear,
Who put the lamp in the fridge, my dear?

And when I thought I'd figured it out,
The phone's a brick, it screams, no doubt.
A dance of chaos, a whirlwind spun,
With no road map, we just run!

A Journey Without a GPS

Off I went on a grand delight,
Maps are useless; I took a flight.
The signs were mixed, I took a chance,
Got lost in thought, forgot to dance.

Finding my way through twists and bends,
Asking a duck, made lots of friends.
Turn left at laughter, right at the fun,
Where's the guidebook? It seems I'm done!

The car ran out, oh what a charade,
Walking in circles, a grand parade!
With ice cream in hand, my fate is sweet,
Lost in the moment, a wondrous feat.

Through puddles and pranks, the world goes round,
With every wrong turn, joy is found.
Forget the map, come rant and rave,
In the journey of hearts, we misbehave!

Lessons in the Unexpected

Woke up late, it's half past ten,
The toast exploded, I tried again.
A sock on the dog, a hat on the cat,
These lessons, oh, they always sat!

In the kitchen, a whirlwind spins,
Cooking chaos, no prize, just sins.
Flour on my nose, and eggs in my hair,
Has anyone seen the guide for this affair?

My plants had a party, all sprouted late,
One made a friend, I thought it was fate.
Watering can? My cup held some tea,
These lessons unravel, so silly and free!

I speak with plants; they share their dreams,
They talk back, or so it seems.
In this dance of blunders, I take a bow,
Expect the unexpected, here and now!

The Tapestry of Unforeseen Threads

Sewed a quilt of hopes and dreams,
But ended up with mismatched seams.
The cat's in the fabric, a playful sprite,
Where's the guide? This doesn't feel right!

Each patch tells tales of joyful flaws,
Stitches zig-zagging without a pause.
A bit of laughter, a dash of glue,
What's missing now? Ah, yes—just you!

In the attic, treasures found,
A box of chaos, all around.
Wrapping mistakes in a shiny thread,
With laughter and love, onward I tread.

Together we weave a colorful jest,
In this tapestry, we are truly blessed.
If we knew the plan, would it still be grand?
In the art of folly, we take a stand!

The Enigma of Everyday Choices

Woke up today, what should I wear?
Socks with stripes? Or more of a flair?
Coffee or tea? Oh, what a duel!
Guess I'll just stand here, looking a fool.

Should I walk left or take the right?
Might end up on a rollercoaster flight!
Should I sing? Should I dance?
Or stare at my ceiling, lost in a trance?

Dinner is tricky, what's on the menu?
Pizza or salad? So hard to construe!
Add a dessert? Now there's a thought!
Maybe just popcorn—who knows what I've caught?

Each day's a puzzle, oh what a treat!
Lost in the choices, so bittersweet.
With every decision, laughter and cheer,
Guess it's just fun not knowing what's near!

Beneath the Shadows of Certainty

Certainty hides like a sneaky cat,
Prowling around, imagine that!
Plans fall apart, like socks in a wash,
Do we follow the path or just splash and nosh?

Seek advice, from a friend or a sage?
But they just chuckle, flipping the page.
"What's your plan?" they ask with a grin,
I shrug, roll my eyes, where to begin?

Should I wear mismatched shoes just for fun?
Heck why not; it's all overrun!
Beneath the layers of safety and fear,
Wiggle your toes, there's nothing to sheer!

In certainty's shade, we dance with despair,
Juggling decisions, yet who even cares?
Laugh at the mess, or what might unfold,
For the wildest tales are the ones never told!

Chasing Shadows in a Tangled Forest

In a forest of choices, I skipped and I hopped,
But every decision just flopped and dropped.
Paths twisted round like spaghetti on plates,
Outsmarted by squirrels, they're perfect at fates.

What's that noise? Is it laughter or fear?
Or just a lost book that's missing a tear?
Maps don't help when you're lost in the fray,
Just follow the giggles, they'll show you the way!

Should I climb that tree or just wave from below?
Is it wise to shout? Or a private show?
Chasing my shadow through brambles and twine,
Who knew a detour could feel so divine?

Embrace the chaos, let whimsy lead you,
For every misstep brings something new!
With trees that chuckle and sunlight that glows,
It's a comedy show that nobody knows!

Fragments of a Fleeting Map

I found a map, all faded and torn,
It promised adventure, a journey reborn.
But the X was a blot, just a random mark,
Where am I headed? Just lost in the dark.

Treasure or trouble? It's hard to discern,
Every path twists like it's ready to turn.
Do I follow the birds or the smell of fresh bread?
Maybe just wander 'til my feet feel lead.

Oh, look! A sign that's barely still there,
"Right to the left" doesn't make sense, I swear!
Should I ask for directions or trust my own lore?
Guess I'll just giggle and explore more and more!

With fragments of maps, I set out to roam,
Each silly detour feels just like home.
So if you find puzzles, don't fret or despair,
Life's most silly moments are full of fresh air!

Instructions Written in Sand

The signs were all there, written in sand,
But a gust of wind had other plans.
We laughed as we tried to understand,
Clueless, we traced with our hands.

The map I drew led nowhere at all,
Like a treasure hunt for a ghost.
We stumbled and fumbled, had a great fall,
At least we could laugh about it the most.

With each step we took, we spiraled and spun,
Like dancers, it seemed, out of sync.
We searched for the rules, but they don't come,
Just a chuckle, a sigh, and a wink.

So here we are, with our quirky guide,
A trail of giggles and mess.
While looking for wisdom, we can't let it slide,
Embrace the chaos, indulge in the jest.

Lost in the Turning Pages

I opened a book hoping for clear sights,
But the chapters just mocked my poor quest.
With riddles and puzzles, it gave me light bites,
As I drooled over thoughts of a nap on a rest.

Each page turned felt like a spin of the wheel,
Hints scattered like confetti in the air.
I laughed out loud, what a strange deal,
Perhaps it's all part of the rare flare.

I wrote a few notes, utterly daft,
Guidelines on how not to be wrong.
But every good laugh comes from the draft,
The answers were missing; I sing my own song.

So here's to the journey, the maze on the run,
Where instruction books vanish like mist.
With humor and folly, we'll still have our fun,
In the pages lost, we find what we missed.

Questions Without Answers

Why do socks vanish into thin air?
What creature dances in the night?
Do fish get thirsty when they swim without care?
And why can't I ever take flight?

As answers elude me, I ponder and stew,
Analyzing mysteries like a detective in place.
What's the deal with those clowns? We've all seen quite a few,
Is there an instruction manual—they're all just a chase?

Perhaps the confusion is meant for our cheer,
With questions spinning like tops in a game.
We navigate chaos, we've nothing to fear,
Embrace the absurd, giggle on blame.

So here's to the queries that spark a good laugh,
To wonders that weave in and out of the light.
In absurdity's grip, we'll still find our path,
What a fun ride—questions take flight!

The Art of Trial and Error

Experimenting daily, a curious fate,
Mixing and matching, it seems like a craze.
I built a new dish that looked second-rate,
But hey, it's the taste that counts in this maze!

With every misstep, I chuckle aloud,
Each failure a gem, a gem made of clay.
I stumbled through recipes, all feeling quite proud,
As the smoke set the fire alarms into play.

I tried to assemble a shelf with great flair,
What's a couple of screws? Just a moment to pause!
Now it's a masterpiece sitting in mid-air,
An abstract creation that broke all the laws.

Oh, the joy in the process—what a grand show,
With laughter and blunders, I always proceed.
In this art of trying, I'll always bestow,
That life finds its color in each silly deed.

Mistakes as Stepping Stones

I tripped on a sock, took a dive,
Thought I was smart, but I barely survived.
Each slip and each fall, a lesson to learn,
Now I embrace blunders, it's my turn!

Coffee spills count as art, don't you see?
Splashed on my shirt, now a stylish me!
Instructions all fuzzy, I scribble instead,
Dancing through chaos, with crumbs in my bed.

The GPS leads me to a wrong place,
But I find hidden gems, and I pick up the pace.
A map made of giggles, with don'ts that I try,
Building my moments, at least I can fly!

Every faux pas a party, oh what a laugh,
Mixed up my plans like a math problem path.
Mistakes aren't just stumbles, they're stepping stones,
Turning my blunders to whimsical tones.

Chaos Beneath the Stars

Under the sky, I lost my way,
Tripped over thoughts on the Milky Way.
Asteroids tumbling, my dreams in a whirl,
But shooting for stars, watch my ambitions swirl!

Aliens chuckle, or maybe it's fate,
As I fumble through life, it feels like a date.
With cosmos so vast, I just have to try,
Floating through chaos, I'm that silly guy.

A nebula's burst, like my morning toast,
Caught in the kitchen, I often boast.
Recipes vague, and directions a blur,
Count this as stellar, I'm a cosmic stir!

So here's to the mayhem, the sparkles, the fun,
Twinkling confusion, all part of the run.
Dancing with stars, let's waltz through the night,
In chaos we find our purest delight.

A Map of Unwritten Paths

A blank piece of paper, where to begin?
No signs, no arrows, just laughter and din.
Paths that are winding, with plot twists anew,
Let me write my story, I'll scribble a clue!

My coffee shop map leads me astray,
But bumping into friends makes the grey go away.
A treasure sought under life's greedy grin,
Each wrong turn's a riddle, let the games begin!

There's no compass to hold, just the heart's gentle sway,
Architect of mayhem, in my own silly way.
The journey unfolds like a wiggly worm,
Who knew the unknown could help us confirm?

So give me the chaos, the fun, and the flair,
I'll carve out my own trail, with laughter to share.
A joyous adventure without the rules,
In this map of mishaps, we sparkle like jewels.

The Art of Asking Questions

Excuse me, dear universe, what's the right way?
I question the clouds, the sun, and the bay.
Is there a manual for when things go wrong?
Why do pancakes flop? And where do they belong?

Do socks migrate? What makes green beans shout?
When do we figure out what life's all about?
Thinking in circles, but laughter I find,
A riddle-filled journey keeps me aligned.

With quizzes of nonsense, I scribble and write,
What's the deal with laundry at two in the night?
A philosopher's dream or a toddler's delight,
The joy's in the questions, so let's take flight!

Who knew that confusion could paint such a smile?
In search of the answers, I'll stay for a while.
Curiosity giggles, in truth I'm a guest,
In this grand sitcom, let's just laugh our best.

When the Compass Fails

I bought a compass, thought it wise,
It spun around, much to my surprise.
I followed north, then turned to east,
Found myself lost at a sandwich feast.

The map I drew was a shaky sort,
A treasure hunt in a local court.
With every step, my doubts increased,
Turns out the 'X' was my favorite feast.

Darts in hand, I made my throw,
Hit a tree, where did that go?
"Adventure!" they said with a grin so wide,
But my adventure was a rollercoaster ride.

Next time I'll skip the compass chat,
And stick to my cat who knows where it's at!
With purrs and nudges, she leads the way,
I won't get lost, at least not today.

In Search of the Lost Guide

I wandered around with a puzzled look,
Searching for answers in a half-baked book.
Every page turned, another laugh,
Who knew my guide was a cheeky giraffe?

It told me to salsa down the street,
With no shoes on, just the rhythm of my feet.
If that's the secret, I'm in for a ride,
Laughing through life while lacking pride.

The route involved coffee, socks, and snacks,
Managed to trip on my own two tracks.
With no map to hold, just vibes to guide,
I found the journey better than the stride.

So here's to the laughs and the wild goose chase,
I'll take missteps at a charming pace.
Let's toast to confusion, my heart in a twirl,
Who needs a guide when I've got this world?

Turning the Blank Pages

I opened the book, just blank and bare,
Flipping through pages without a care.
A suggestion to draw, so I scribbled a fish,
Wished for wisdom, but got my own swish.

With crayons in hand, I made it quite bright,
A masterpiece lost in the depths of night.
A unicorn dancing on a slice of cake,
That's when I knew, my sanity's at stake.

Scratched notes and doodles in every line,
A puzzle of nonsense I thought was divine.
Through chaos, I chuckle, a vibrant spree,
Each blank page whispers, "Just be free!"

So let's keep spinning the stories galore,
With sketches and giggles, I'll explore!
In the book of life, let's scribble and play,
Who needs directions? Let's wing it today!

Scribbled Notes in the Margins

Found some notes in my pocket today,
A shopping list turned to a twisty ballet.
"Don't forget laughter!" my scribbles declare,
And new socks—though I'm not sure where.

Each margin bursting with wild ideas,
About dancing under a shower of cheers.
"A nap here, a snack there, embrace the weird,"
These forgotten thoughts are now greatly revered.

Every scribble tells tales so bold,
Of wild adventures, both young and old.
Who knew my notes would lead me to fun?
With margins clearer than the rising sun!

So I'll keep my notes, my awkward prose,
As reminders that life's not a straightforward dose.
In the grand scheme, let's chuckle and jest,
With each little note, I feel truly blessed.

The Orchestra of Chance Encounters

In the symphony of random spots,
We dance like penguins, tying knots.
A wink, a smile, a serendipitous play,
Who knew missteps could lead us this way?

With pizza slices and lost dog barks,
We harmonize in this circus of larks.
Trombones blare and the kazoo's in tune,
As we juggle our dreams under the moon.

Yet, as the clock ticks in its silly spree,
We question what we missed, what could be.
Is there a manual for this wacky stroll?
Or just the thrill of not being in control?

So grab your hat, and spin around,
In this quirky show, laughter's the sound.
With every twist in our playful fate,
Who needs instructions when you can create?

Pages Torn and Rewritten

I found a diary buried deep,
With messy notes and secrets to keep.
Each page crumpled, like a pie fight gone wrong,
A script for a show where we all sing along.

The plot thickens with a coffee stain,
Adventures scribbled on a passing train.
Lost in the margins, a joke or two,
Why write the rules when chaos is due?

A chapter ends with a twisty grin,
As laughter erupts from where we've been.
We rewrite the script on dinner napkins,
Finding joy in the mess of our actions.

The book might be torn, with pages askew,
But it's full of wisdom, quirky and true.
So we pen our mishaps and misadventures vast,
For who needs a guide when we're having a blast?

Echoes of Unheard Voices

Here in the chatter of the everyday grind,
I hear whispers, the fun kind.
A sock's rebellion, a cat's demand,
Unheard voices lend a helping hand.

As the toaster pops in a quirky burst,
It joins the chorus, ready to jibe and flirt.
In the ruckus of life's mundane show,
We find the jokes, the chuckles flow.

Hidden in gaps, with friends on speed dial,
A clown in the corner, turning every trial.
The wise words of socks draped on the floor,
Who knew the echoes could open a door?

So raise a glass to the unseen and felt,
For in this weird mess, laughter's dealt.
Let's savor the chatter, the silenced cheer,
As we spin our tales, it's all about the dear!

Choosing Paths Unforeseen

With a fork in the road and a fork on my plate,
I'm torn between salad and something great.
Should I take the path not often trod?
Or ace the pizza slice—my own little god?

Each option glimmers, a shiny delight,
Potato chips whisper, 'Take a bite!'
Yet, here I wander, lost in the stew,
Wondering where these choices will lead me to.

A tap dance on schedules, a two-step of plans,
With celery sticks and jelly beans in hands.
But every detour's a chance to explore,
Where's the manual? I think I'll ignore.

So let's skip the rules and chart our own quest,
Where laughter is king and fun is the best.
In this grand adventure of hops and skips,
Here's to uncertainty and tasty trips!

Unfolding Amidst the Uncertain

Why does the toaster burn toast?
Should I blame it on the ghost?
Cooking rules? I toss them away,
Just wing it and hope it's okay.

Directions lost on a winding street,
I find more snacks than I find my seat.
Maps are for others, not for me,
I'll dance to my own symphony.

Advice from friends rolls off my back,
While I stumble through the life I lack.
But laughter echoes through each blunder,
Finding joy in the wild thunder.

Turns out humor's the best GPS,
Helping me cope when things are a mess.
So here's to chaos, carefree and bright,
Navigating wrongs that often feel right.

A Road of Serendipitous Findings

Driving blind with no clear map,
Joyfully tripping, oh, what a hap!
Curveballs fly with every turn,
Yet I laugh and refuse to yearn.

Coffee spills and shoes untied,
Every misstep feels like a ride.
Who needs rules when there's fun to find?
Each little mishap's a joy to unwind.

Should I wear socks with sandals today?
Maybe eat dessert first—hey, why not sway?
Life's a circus, a charming spree,
With surprises waiting around every tree.

So grab a snack and let's go free,
With no instruction, just you and me.
Let's tumble through the good and bad,
And savor the moments that make us glad.

The Unfolding Narrative of Now

What's the script to this crazy show?
Not a clue, but come join the flow!
I get my cues from dancing cats,
With life's plot twists, we're all like that.

Spilling drinks while cracking jokes,
In this play, the fridge still croaks.
From fumbles to flops, it's all a blast,
Here's a wink to the future and a nod to the past.

Why follow a path when you can stray?
To dodge the crowd and just sway your way!
With each scene, I'm crafting my role,
Fueled by giggles, I've found my soul.

So here's to the now—imperfect and grand,
With my trusty sidekick, fate's gentle hand.
Let's write our tales in colors bold,
In this wild story yet to unfold.

The Unmapped Territory of Being

Welcome to my uncharted land,
Where rules go awry and smiles are planned.
This road ahead—an unscripted thrill,
Grab your courage, it's time to chill.

Why fit in when you can stand out?
Shouting "Eureka!" with a little doubt.
Each stumble's a step, a twist of fate,
In this madness, activities await.

Is this the way to where I need to go?
I've misplaced my map—just follow the flow!
Bump into joy as it springs from the ground,
In this wild tangle, true peace is found.

So dance through the shadows, sing in the light,
In the unmapped chaos, find your delight.
For it's not about where the path leads us,
But the fun we have—as we ride this bus.

Footnotes to Our Existence

We stumble through days like clumsy clowns,
With mismatched socks and runaway frowns.
Instructions are missing, or maybe misplaced,
As we navigate chaos with pie on our face.

Each joy comes with wrinkles of sweet little pain,
Like stepping in gum while it starts to rain.
We laugh at our quirks, embrace all the quirks,
While dodging the hurdles and odd little quirks.

Try to read signs but they all look the same,
Like a game with no rules, yet we're all in the frame.
With footnotes and scribbles scrawled in broken prose,
We sketch out a plan that nobody knows.

So flip through the pages, they're filled with surprise,
Our handbook's a joke, yet it opens our eyes.
In this messy adventure, we dance and we spin,
With a smile and a wink, let the madness begin!

Manual for the Heart

If love had a manual, it'd win a prize,
Filled with heart charts and elephant-sized sighs.
But no glossy pages with tips for the soul,
Just the chaos of crushes and yearning for Whole.

It'd say, 'Be brave, but don't jump too high,'
As you land with a thud and a comical cry.
With half-hearted advice that'll leave you in stitches,
And warnings 'bout feelings that come with some
glitches.

Hearts come with quirks, like pets in a cage,
Their moods change like seasons—a never-ending stage.
Borrowed from movies, the lines all go wrong,
But who needs a manual when we have this song?

So let's skip the instructions, just dance with the beat,
And if we trip over it, hey, isn't that sweet?
In this comedy show of likes and of hearts,
The manual is laughter, that's where it all starts!

A Compass in the Dark

When shadows loom large, and the path disappears,
We fumble for guidance, suppressing our fears.
With stars in our eyes and a laugh on our lips,
We navigate darkness with questionable trips.

Where's the map for this maze that's sewn shut?
But we'll take a detour, embrace every rut.
With a compass that's spinning like a rollercoaster,
We'll aim for the joy, with fate as our hoster.

Through giggles and gigabytes of trial and error,
We find laughter's light is a fabulous bearer.
So when life gets confusing, just give it a wink,
With a swish and a swirl, you'll know how to think.

A compass may fail, but a smile's the key,
To wander through darkness, well, can't you see?
In the wild of our journey, let humour ignite,
For every misstep makes the stories more bright!

The Script We Never Received

We're actors in a play, no script in our hands,
Throwing random lines like improvised bands.
With cues that are missed and props left to chance,
We embrace the absurdity, a clumsy romance.

Who wrote this weird script that's gone all astray?
With plot twists and turns that lead us away.
From misplaced beginnings to endings unclear,
We're the stars of a drama filled with silly cheer.

Ad-libbing through moments, while laughter doth reign,
As we dance on the stage and escape from the mundane.
The audience chuckles, on every mishap,
They cheer for each stutter, each folly—a flap!

So let's raise our voices, embrace the unknown,
For the best kind of stories are those that we own.
With joy in the chaos and fun in the mess,
We'll write our own verses, and oh, what a bless!

Unpacking the Unwritten Script

In the drawer, I find a sock,
But 'why's the puppy in the clock?'
A manual's missing for this spree,
Guess I'll just wing it—who needs a key?

My friend insists on maps and charts,
Yet trips go off with silly starts.
I spill my drink and laugh at fate,
Who knew clumsiness could feel so great?

Instructions vague, like breadcrumbs tossed,
With every step, my path gets crossed.
I juggle chaos, that's my game,
With floppy hats and silly names.

So here's to all who dance unplanned,
With mismatched shoes and coffee cans.
We write the script with joyful cheer,
A story bold, year after year.

Against the Current of Expectations

They said to follow the conventional route,
I took a detour, a silly shout.
Who needs directions or a guide?
I'd rather sail the whimsy tide.

My GPS broke, the signal's lost,
I'm eating pancakes while I'm crossed.
Expectations float like bubbles, dear,
I'll prance in puddles, have no fear.

The road looked straight, but oh, surprise!
A rubber duck floats by, what a prize!
I'll throw confetti in the air,
And see who joins this wild affair.

Against the current, I swim with glee,
Navigating chaos, so carefree.
So raise a toast, let's sing out loud,
To those who laugh and stand unbowed.

The Journey's Unseen Artistry

With paintbrushes of whimsy, we start to scribble,
Each choice a splash, each laugh a giggle.
Colors blend where mishaps lay,
In this wacky dance, I'm led astray.

A traffic jam? Just a chance to play,
I turn up the tunes and sway the day.
Brush strokes wide, with splatters bright,
Creating chaos feels so right.

I paint my worries with shades of fun,
Celebrating blunders on the run.
Mistakes like stars, they light my path,
With quirky giggles and silly math.

So here's to artistry on every route,
Where laughter reigns and doubt's in doubt.
We navigate the fun unseen,
A masterpiece in every dream.

Foundations Built on Curiosity

I built a tower out of books,
My only tool? A playful look.
Curiosity's spark, my guiding light,
Each question bounces, a silly sight.

They said, 'Don't touch the cookie jar!'
But oops, I reached; now there's a scar.
Taste testing truths, I spar and romp,
With crumbs of wisdom, I proudly stomp.

Foundations wobbly, yet here I stand,
Crafting castles made of sand.
My curious heart, a wild card,
Life's little quirks don't hit too hard.

So let's embrace the twists and turns,
In every stumble, the spirit learns.
With laughter as our sturdy glue,
We'll build a world anew, it's true!